A TIME TO LOVE

A TIME TO LOVE

Love Poems
for
Today

EDITED AND ILLUSTRATED BY

JOAN BERG VICTOR

CROWN PUBLISHERS, INC., NEW YORK

PRINTED IN THE UNITED STATES OF AMERICA
PUBLISHED SIMULTANEOUSLY IN CANADA
BY GENERAL PUBLISHING COMPANY LIMITED
Fifth Printing, January, 1975

Acknowledgments

The author gratefully acknowledges permission to use the following copyrighted material.

"Now and Then" by Arlo Guthrie. © copyright 1967, 1969 by Appleseed Music Inc.
   All rights reserved. Used by pemission.

"Love Pieces" by Richard Eberhart. From *Shifts of Being* by Richard Eberhart. © 1968
   by Richard Eberhart.

"Love Is" by May Swenson. Copyright 1949 May Swenson. Reprinted by permission of
   Charles Scribner's Sons from *To Mix with Time* by May Swenson.

"The Jealous Lovers" by Donald Hall. From *The Alligator Bride: Poems New and Selected*
   by Donald Hall. Copyright © 1963 by Donald Hall. Originally appeared in *The New Yorker*
   and reprinted by permission of Harper & Row, Publishers, Inc.

"One Question" by Eli Siegel. Definition Press for "One Question," by Eli Siegel, from
   Hot Afternoons Have Been in Montana: Poems, copyright © 1953, 1954, 1957, by Eli Siegel.

"If I Were Paris" by James Weldon Johnson. From *Saint Peter Relates an Incident* by James Weldon
   Johnson. Copyright 1935 by James Weldon Johnson, copyright © renewed 1963 by
   Grace Nail Johnson. Reprinted by permission of The Viking Press, Inc.

"Have I Given You a Valentine Lately?" by Lois Wyse. Reprinted by permission of The World
   Publishing Company from *I Love You Better Now* by Lois Wyse. Copyright © 1970 by
   The World Publishing Company.

"Beauty Never Old" by James Weldon Johnson. From *Saint Peter Relates an Incident* by
   James Weldon Johnson. Copyright 1917 by James Weldon Johnson. All rights reserved.
   Reprinted by permission of The Viking Press, Inc.

"Love Song" by William Carlos Williams. From *Collected Earlier Poems*, by William Carlos Williams.
   Copyright 1938 by William Carlos Williams. Reprinted by permission of New Directions
   Publishing Corporation.

"We Love" by Ted Bluechel, Jr. © Copyright 1967 Beechwood Music Corporation.

"Once I Loved" by Rod McKuen from *In Someone Else's Shadow*. Copyright © 1968 Editions
   Chanson Co.

I thank Cary and Havlock, Cathy
and Amy, Gary and Dan.
And I thank Richard, Daniel, and Elizabeth
and my parents
for sharing with me
the secret of life—love.

Contents

A TIME TO LOVE

A Time to Love

In today's world of stirrings to become . . .
of trying to find a place in the
too-rapidly changing macrocosm, we
tend to forget the quiet word LOVE—
that love today is quite the same
as the word and the meaning one thousand
years ago. Certain truths are timeless,
certain beliefs need never change. I
have tried to show this in this collection.
The secret of life is love, today, yesterday,
tomorrow.

—Joan Berg Victor

Prologue

To everything there is a season,
And a time to every purpose under the heaven:
A time to be born, and a time to die;
A time to plant, and a time to pluck up that which is planted;
A time to kill, and a time to heal;
A time to break down, and a time to build up;
A time to weep, and a time to laugh;
A time to mourn, and a time to dance;
A time to cast away stones, and a time to gather stones together;
A time to embrace, and a time to refrain from embracing;
A time to get, and a time to lose;
A time to keep, and a time to cast away;
A time to rend, and a time to sew;
A time to keep silence, and a time to speak;
A time to love, and a time to hate;
A time of war, and a time of peace.

—Ecclesiastes, Chapter 3

Daybreak

At dawn she lay with her profile at that angle
Which, when she sleeps, seems the carved face of an angel.
Her hair a harp, the hand of a breeze follows
And plays, against the white cloud of the pillows.
Then, in a flush of rose, she woke, and her eyes that opened
Swam in blue through her rose flesh that dawned.
From her dew of lips, the drop of one word
Fell like the first of fountains: murmured
"Darling," upon my ears the song of the first bird.
"My dream becomes my dream," she said, "come true.
I waken from you to my dream of you."
Oh, my own wakened dream that dared assume
The audacity of her sleep. Our dreams
Poured into each other's arms, like streams.

—Stephen Spender

Now and Then

Hello again. The mornin' dawn
has burned away the midnight mist.
Now and then I feel so fine,
and now and then I don't feel lonely,
now and then and only in my mind.
I want to go outside today,
go away,
I think I'll stay.
Now and then I talk with you,
and now and then you turn me on,
now and then and when
I don't feel blue.
Ah maybe I could tell you now
that I really love you.
Please do understand that you are there
in the air.
Now and then you turn me on,
now and then you must be gone,
now and then I said, "Say so long,
now and forever." Then—

—Arlo Guthrie

Love Pieces

I

Love Come Again

You are the poetry of the world
Always climbing up beyond it
To a purity beyond words,
Love so great it can only touch,

Can only touch in so much joy
At the edge of radiancy beyond it,
Never possess the whole meaning,
No words are secret enough, deep enough.

When we, startled, see face to face
Love itself brought to life by chance,
The catch in the breath, the look in the eye,
We cannot believe in our senses

Directed by so much ravishment,
Being so taken up in ancient mystery.
Love! Love! It is impossible, it cannot be!
And caress the flesh as if time could never die.

II

I want to write of the death of love
And of the love of death
For surely love shall die and death shall live.

When love is in the ascendant,
Influence of brightness in total rapture,
No lover can think of the death of love.

He sheds the dark garments of life
And lives in a radiancy of the flesh
As if this were a sovereign rite of gold.

He lives in glory and he lives in truth,
The world becomes a greatness of love
For which he can find no adequate words.

It is the luminescence of the impossible
Become possible, it is the evident strangeness
Of a gift of the gods to human believers.

It is the testament of the deep midnight
And it is the totality of experience,
So it seems in strangeness and benediction.

It is richness of ambivalence thrown away,
The triumph of life over ambiguity,
Total defeat of irony. It seems drossless,

The expression of an extravagant estate,
Ultimate in the ineffable, beyond speech
When feeling has the mastery of life.

I celebrate this paradise of the senses
As the only paradise, and not of the mind.
Then the mind persists to bring love down.

An unbearable bleakness claims the day,
Harshness, suffering, disorder, war and pain.
Fate goes against the love of man.

I want to write of the death of love
And of the love of death,
For surely love shall die and death shall live.

—*Richard Eberhart*

Love Is

a rain of diamonds
in the mind

the soul's fruit
sliced in two

a dark spring
loosed at the lips of light

under-earth waters
unlocked from their lurking
to sparkle in a crevice
parted by the sun

a temple
not of stone but cloud
beyond the heart's roar
and all violence

outside the anvil-stunned domain
unfrenzied space

between the grains of change
blue permanence

one short step
to the good ground

the bite into bread again

—*May Swenson*

12

The Jealous Lovers

When he lies in the night away from her
the backs of his eyelids burn.
He turns in the darkness as if it were an oven.
The flesh parches and he lies awake
thinking of everything wrong.

He remembers the name of a man
and a weekend before they loved each other.
His mind in its tight corner
watches a scene by the ocean last summer.
Or is it next summer he watches?

In the morning when he goes to meet her,
his heart struggles at his ribs
like an animal trapped in its burrow.
Then he sees her running to meet him,
red-faced with hurry and cold.

She stumbles over the snow.
Her knees above orange knee-socks
bob in a froth of the hems
of skirt and coat and petticoat.
Her eyes have not shut all night.

—Donald Hall

14

Thank You

All the taxi horns have sounded their retreat.
The wind is down to nothing but a whisper in the
         street.
And now as you lie sleeping I'll take
a moment just to tell you
all the things I never say when you're awake.

Thank you for the raspberries this morning
and thank you for the orange marmalade.
And last night let me say
when you might have gone away
thank you very much because you stayed.

Thank you for the sun you brought this morning
even though the sky was full of clouds.
And thank you for the way
you held me yesterday
and steered me through the noisy Paris crowds.

I can't look ahead to the future
and I'm too old to run home to the past.
So now while you sleep on beside me
I'll do what I can to make this moment last.

Thank you for another special morning
and thank you for an even better day.
And thank you in advance
if there's even half a chance you'll stay,
one more morning. One more day.

—Rod McKuen

16

One Question

I—
Why?

—*Eli Siegel*

If I Were Paris

Not for me the budding girl
Or the maiden in full bloom,
Sure of beauty and of charm,
Careless of the distant doom,
Laughing in the face of years
That stretch out so long and far,
Mindful of the things to be,
Heedless of the things that are;

But the woman sweetly ripe,
Under the autumn of her skies;
Thin lines of care about her mouth,
And utterless longings in her eyes.

—James Weldon Johnson

20

Have I Given You a Valentine Lately?

I don't believe in Valentines.
They are young and vulnerable
And hopelessly old-fashioned.

Valentines are for
Sentimental sentimentalists,
Romantic romantics,
And those who still believe in
Happy endings.

I am at that point in life
When I know how the story ends
And when the nights grow cold.
So I do not expect
Lace slips,
Surprise trips,
Cherry flips,
Or tender little poems
Because it is That Day.

Instead I want my Valentines
At unexpected times.
I want to know you think of me
In mid-May, March, and June.
For I believe,
My dear,
One day a year
Is not enough for love.

—*Lois Wyse*

Beauty Never Old

When buffeted and beaten by life's storms,
When by the bitterness of life oppressed,
I need no surer haven than your arms,
I want no happier shelter than your breast.

When over my way there falls the sudden blight
Of sunless days and nights of starless skies,
Enough for me the ever-steadfast light
I know is always shining in your eyes.

The world, for me,
And all the world can hold
Is circled by your arms;
For me there lies
Within the lighted shadows of your eyes
The only beauty that is never old.

—*James Weldon Johnson*

24

Love Song

What have I to say to you
When we shall meet?
Yet—
I lie here thinking of you.

The stain of love
Is upon the world!
Yellow, yellow, yellow
It eats into the leaves,
Smears with saffron
The horned branches that lean
Heavily
Against a smooth purple sky!

There is no light
Only a honey-thick stain
That drips from leaf to leaf
And limb to limb
Spoiling the colors
Of the whole world—

I am alone.
The weight of love
Has buoyed me up
Till my head
Knocks against the sky.

See me!
My hair is dripping with nectar—
Starlings carry it
On their black wings.

See, at last
My arms and my hands
Are lying idle.

How can I tell
If I shall ever love you again
As I do now?

—William Carlos Williams

26

We Love

I wake her, I hold her
I tell her I love her
and she smiles and says the same.
She makes me feel like sunshine when she says my name.
Her laughing, her crying,
her caring, her sharing
of my life means more to me
than all the wealth and fame that fortune brings to me.
Turn your head around—
Are you sure love's the feeling that surrounds you?
Does the question count when you feel good,
as good inside as I do, do you?
The sun sets—

—Ted Bluechel, Jr.

28

Once I Loved

for Greta Keller

Once I loved the wind as it blew
down from the mountains over the land.
Once I loved the touch of the sun
almost as much as the touch of a hand.

And once I loved the smell of the sea,
the feel of the waves rolling over me.
Sea and sand, air and sky,
Once I loved, once I loved.

Once I loved all of God's things
that grow on the earth and cover the land.
Air and sky, sea and sand,
Once I loved but never till now.

—Rod McKuen

To Mary

The words of love in this our time
Are fouled with advertisers' slime,
Besides whatever matter sticks
From movies, television, and slicks.

Even the poet with all his art
Speaks words no cleaner than his heart:
And seize each word and rub it clean,
It still wears the face of the go-between.

Though rivaling gilded monument,
Shakespeare's rhyme, for all that, bent
In the final couplet's flattery
The pregnant hinges of the knee.

Shelley sighed and swooned, and yet
Deserted poor foolish Harriet;
And Herrick sang Electra and, in a
Strain as sweet, Julia, Anthea, Myrha,
      Perilla, Sapho, and Corinna.

Tender Rossetti so humbly buried
His poems with the love he'd married,
And heartbroken sorrowed—but then
Vanity dug them up again.

This sermon in these poor verses lies:
To be charitable, to be wise,
To take my love in silent deed,
To give in measure with my need.

—Samuel Yellen

Song Without Words

I wanted to write you some words you'd remember
words so alert they'd leap from the paper
and crawl up your shoulder and lie by your ears
and be there to comfort you down through the years.
But it was cloudy that day and I was lazy
and so I stayed in bed just thinking about it.

I wanted to write you and tell you that maybe
love songs from lovers are unnecessary.
We are what we feel and writing it down
seems foolish sometimes without vocal sound.
But I spent the day drinking coffee, smoking
        cigarettes
and looking in the mirror practicing my smile.

I wanted to write you one last, long love song
that said what I feel one final time.
Not comparing your eyes and mouth to the stars
but telling you only how like yourself you are.
But by the time I thought of it, found a pen,
put the pen to ink, the ink to paper,
you were gone.

And so, this song has no words.

—Rod McKuen

The Woman at the Spring Drip

Always running, always there,
the pipe end brought from the hill
drips into the green lair
of the trough, the center a dull
eye, an eye.

And I, day in, day out,
hear the water run to the rim,
I hear the sound louden
like the voice of him
I loved, I loved.

He bathed his head in the drip,
he drank at the cold tap
when the summer was hot.
Now he is gone
and I am not, I am not.

—*Millen Brand*

36

If Where You Walk

If where you walk,
Morning glories should unfurl
Their trumpets of blue silk
And play a joyous music
I would not be surprised.
If at your passing glance
Angels made of stone
Would shake wakened wings, and
Gargoyles somersault with gladness,
I would not disbelieve.
I know your magic, too.

—Anonymous

Separation

While I waited for that line worth listening for
you searched for something else   I found no use
in the words you spoke   We met for food
I had forgotten to notice   abstractedly ate
finding there was never time to be anything but late
Only at night could I spare a thought for those fingers
limp along the sheet   but your breath was wordless
So   as you sit there opposite saying "Glad
you are happy   I'll always be fond   Yes
I'm all right"   I listen and know I am too late
again.   I hear and feel   but you dare not step nearer
and I   knowing our distance doubled   hesitate—
for   since you no longer move or breathe beside me
I have not found a word worth listening for

—*Keith Barnes*

40

Poems for Marthe

Marthe Away

All night I lay awake beside you,
Leaning on my elbow, watching your
Sleeping face, that face whose purity
Never ceases to astonish me.
I could not sleep. But I did not want
Sleep nor miss it. Against my body,
Your body lay like a warm soft star.
How many nights I have waked and watched
You, in how many places. Who knows?
This night might be the last one of all.
As on so many nights, once more I
Drank from your sleeping flesh the deep still
Communion I am not always strong
Enough to take from you waking, the peace of love.
Foggy lights moved over the ceiling
Of our room, so like the rooms of France
And Italy, rooms of honeymoon,
And gave your face an ever changing
Speech, the secret communication
Of untellable love. I knew then,

As your secret spoke, my secret self,
The blind bird, hardly visible in
An endless web of lies. And I knew
The web too, its every knot and strand,
The hidden crippled bird, the terrible web.
Towards the end of night, as trucks rumbled
In the streets, you stirred, cuddled to me,
And spoke my name. Your voice was the voice
Of a girl who had never known loss
Of love, betrayal, mistrust, or lie.
And later you turned again and clutched
My hand and pressed it to your body.
Now I know surely and forever,
However much I have blotted our
Waking love, its memory is still
There. And I know the web, the net,
The blind and crippled bird. For then, for
One brief instant it was not blind, nor
Trapped, nor crippled. For one heart beat the
Heart was free and moved itself. O love,
I who am lost and damned with words,
Whose words are a business and an art,
I have no words. These words, this poem, this
Is all confusion and ignorance.
But I know that coached by your sweet heart,
My heart beat one free beat and sent
Through all my flesh the blood of truth.

Quietly

Lying here quietly beside you,
My cheek against your firm, quiet thighs,
The calm music of Boccherini
Washing over us in the quiet,
As the sun leaves the housetops and goes
Out over the Pacific, quiet—
So quiet the sun moves beyond us,
So quiet as the sun always goes,
So quiet, our bodies, worn with the
Times and the penances of love, our
Brains curled, quiet in their shells, dormant,
Our hearts slow, quiet, reliable
In their interlocked rhythms, the pulse
In your thigh caressing my cheek. Quiet.

Marthe Growing

Who are you? Who am I? Haunted
By the dead, by the dead and the past and the
Falling inertia of unreal, dead
Men and things. Haunted by the threat
Of the impersonal, that which
Never will admit the person,
The closed world of things. Who are
You? Coming up out of the
Mineral earth, one pale leaf
Unlike any other unfolding,
And then another, strange, new,
Utterly different, nothing
I ever expected, growing
Up out of my warm heart's blood.
All new, all strange, all different.
Your own leaf pattern, your own
Flower and fruit, but fed from
One root, the root of our fused flesh.
I and thou, from the one to
The dual, from the dual
To the other, the wonderful,
Unending, unfathomable
Process of becoming each
Our selves for each other.

A Dialogue of Watching

Let me celebrate you. I
Have never known anyone
More beautiful than you. I
Walking beside you, watching
You move beside me, watching
That still grace of hand and thigh,
Watching your face change with words
You do not say, watching your
Solemn eyes as they turn to me,
Or turn inward, full of knowing,
Slow or quick, watching your full
Lips part and smile or turn grave,
Watching your narrow waist, your
Proud buttocks in their grace, like
A sailing swan, an animal,
Free, your own, and never
To be subjugated, but
Abandoned, as I am to you,
Overhearing your perfect
Speech of motion, of love and
Trust and security as
You feed or play with our children.
I have never known any
One more beautiful than you.

—Kenneth Rexroth

Beautiful You Are

Cathedral evening, tinkle of candles
On the frosted air
Beautiful you are
Beautiful your eyes, lips, hair

Ah, still they come

Evenings like chalices
Where little roofs and trees drink
Until a rude hand
Shatters them, one by one

O beautiful you are

My own
Land of holiness, unblemished grace
Springtime
In this winter place
O in the candles there
More beautiful
Than any legend's face

Your eyes, your hair

—Kenneth Patchen

48

I Love You Better Now

Part I

Before I was in love with you,
I was in love with love.
Oh, what a lovely love
Of cloudless climes and starry skies
With a man that never was.

    This was me.
    The me who lived with girly girl beliefs
    When first she lived with you
    Until little by little,
    Slice by slice,
    Like the layers of wallpaper
    In a hundred-year-old house
    You stripped the pink dreams down.
        Off with the cabbage roses.
        Down with the merry maids.

Backward turns the clock.

Where does reality begin?
When did you peel the last old pattern
And find there really was a woman
Under such a lot of girl?

—*Lois Wyse*

I Love You Better Now

Part II

There it was.
>   Half a sandwich,
>   Lukewarm drink.
The remnants of your lonely lunch.

And as I cleaned
The scrips and scraps
I came across a note you wrote.
A note that was not meant for me.
A scribble of some random thoughts.

And in the margin of the note
I saw my name
Hatched and scratched
In some unconscious half-time.

I put the little paper
In the pocket of my skirt
And each time I touch it
I know well
That I would rather gather
Half your time
And half your thoughts
Than all
Of any other man.

—*Lois Wyse*

52

The Hounded Lovers

Where shall we go?
Where shall we go
    who are in love?

Juliet went
to Friar Laurence's cell
    but we have no rest—

Rain water lies on
the hard ground reflecting
    the morning sky

But where shall we go?
We cannot resolve ourselves
    into a dew

nor sink into the earth.
Shall we postpone it
    to Eternity?

The dry heads of the
golden rod
    turned to stiff ghosts

jerk at their stalks
signaling grave warning.
    Where shall we go?

The movement of benediction
does not turn back
    the cold wind.

      —William Carlos Williams

54

Travel

Loving you, flesh to flesh, I often thought
Of traveling penniless to some mud throne
Where a master might instruct me how to plot
My life away from pain, to love alone
In the bruiseless embrace of stone and lake.

• • •

Now
I know why many men have stopped and wept
Half-way between loves they leave and seek
And wondered if travel leads them anywhere—
Horizons keep the soft line of your cheek,
The windy sky's a locket for your hair.

—*Leonard Cohen*

Our Dread to Speak Our Love

Our dread to speak our love is like
The overwhelming fear a latch
Has for the probing key, that night
Has for the struck, revealing match.

—Paul Engle

By Love We Grow

By love we grow both tenderer and tougher,
Teaching us to delight, and how to suffer.
The pointed nail discovers its true good
Under the hammer driving it into wood.

—*Paul Engle*

58

The Quarrel

Suddenly, after the quarrel, while we waited,
Disheartened, silent, with downcast looks, nor stirred
Eyelid nor finger, hopeless both, yet hoping
Against all hope to unsay the sundering word:

While all the room's stillness deepened, deepened about us,
And each of us crept his thought's way to discover
How, with as little sound as the fall of a leaf,
The shadow had fallen, and lover quarreled with lover;

And while in the quiet I marveled—alas, alas—
At your deep beauty, your tragic beauty, torn
As the pale flower is torn by the wanton sparrow—
This beauty, pitied and loved, and now forsworn;

It was then, when the instant darkened to it darkest,—
When faith was lost with hope, and the rain conspired
To strike its gray arpeggios against our heartstrings,—
When love no longer dared, and scarcely desired:

It was then that suddenly, in the neighbor's room,
The music started: that brave quartet of strings
Breaking out of the stillness, as out of our stillness,
Like the indomitable heart of life that sings

When all is lost; and startled from our sorrow,
Tranced from our grief by that diviner grief,
We raised remembering eyes, each looked at other,
Blinded with tears of joy; and another leaf

Fell silently as that first; and in the instant
The shadow had gone, our quarrel became absurd;
And we rose, to the angelic voices of the music,
And I touched your hand, and we kissed, without a word.

—Conrad Aiken

Whole Love

Every choice is always the wrong choice,
Every vote cast is always cast away—
How can truth hover between alternatives?

Then love me more than dearly, love me wholly,
Love me with no weighing of circumstance,
As I am pledged in honor to love you:

With no weakness, with no speculation
On what might happen should you and I prove less
Than bringers-to-be of our own certainty.
Neither was born by hazard: each foreknew
The extreme possession we are grown into.

—*Robert Graves*

Notes

Butterfly trembles when the wind blows.
You walk near me.
The dog barks at the loud moon.
When you come to me,
I speak softly, softly,
Until we are silent together.
For two hundred years
This pine tree has been trained to grow sideways.
I have known you only one week,
But I bend as you walk toward me.

—Paul Engle

Bedtime

We are a meadow where the bees hum,
mind and body are almost one

as the fire snaps in the stove
and our eyes close,

and mouth to mouth, the covers
pulled over our shoulders,

we drowse as horses drowse afield,
in accord; though the fall cold

surrounds our warm bed, and though
by day we are singular and often lonely.

—Denise Levertov

That Other World

Fatedly alone with you once more
As before time first creaked:
Sole woman and sole man.

Others admire us as we walk this world:
We show them kindliness and mercy,
So be it none grow jealous
Of the truth that echoes between us two,
Or of that other world, in the world's cradle,
Child of your love for me.

—Robert Graves

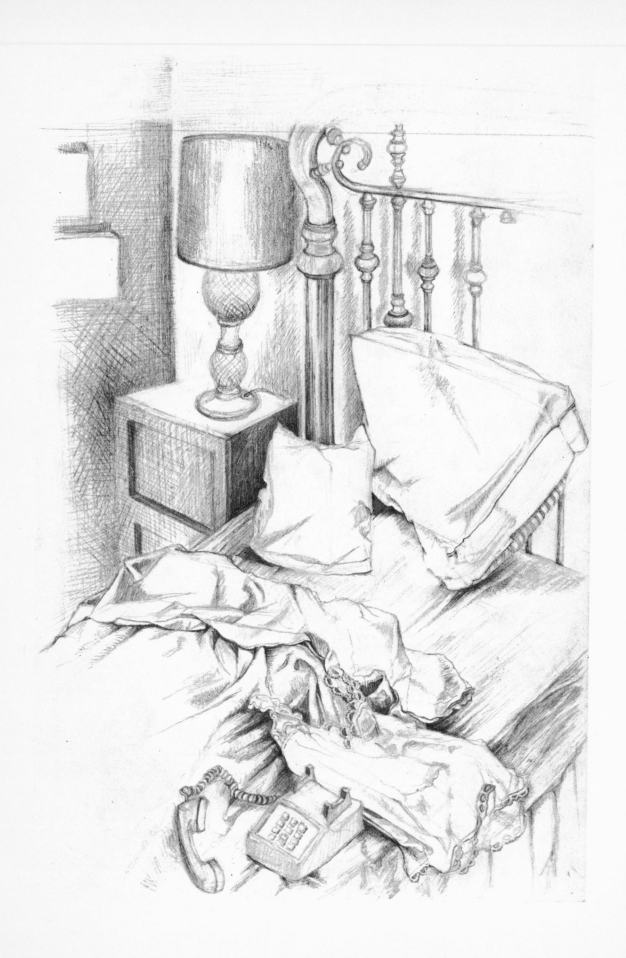

She Has Gone Away

She has gone away with the day
My love has,
Taken all the light colors
All the white clouds.
The wind remains
With shadows and coal dust.

She stayed away all night
My love did,
Hid with the sunset behind the dark.
Now I watch for her at my window
On different days,
Watch until the night returns.

—Hy Sobiloff

Need

What do we need for love—a midnight fire
Flinging itself by fistfuls up the chimney
In soft bright snatches? Do we need the snow,
Gentle as silence, covering the scars
Of weeks of hunger, years of shabby having?
Summer or winter? A heaven of stars? A room?
The smiling mouth, the sadness of desire
Are everywhere the same. If lovers go
Along an unknown road, they find no less
What is familiar. Let them stay at home,
And all will still be strange. This they know
Who with each heartbeat fight the fear of change.

—Babette Deutsch

Dogma

Love is not true: mathematicians know
Truth, that's alive in heaven, and in the mind—
Out of our bodies; you will never find
Love strict as number, and enduring so.
It is not free: alone the grave's narrower
Than the little space in which this passion moves,
With a door that opens inward: he who loves
Measures his paces like a prisoner.

They who give it large names are liars, or
They are fools. More softly, you and I,
Slow to assert what we can never prove,
Wonder what algebraist, what dictator
Can teach us much of truth or tyranny.
Look at me. Do not speak. But this is love.

—Babette Deutsch

As Birds Are
Fitted to the Boughs

As birds are fitted to the boughs
That blossom on the tree
And whisper when the south wind blows—
So was my love to me.

And still she blossoms in my mind
And whispers softly, though
The clouds are fitted to the wind,
The wind is to the snow.

—*Louis Simpson*

The Faithful Lover

I hesitate to write about the spring;
There is a fear with all that loveliness,
A wilderness I feel in everything.

Though not alone, I think of loneliness,
Of God's late isolation in the sky,
Of wisdom turned despair, not happiness.

And while we are together, you and I,
Abandon promises of future bliss,
But love me with the truth now in your eye:

Regard the early falling leaf—a kiss
Regard fidelity a passing thing.
(It gives me courage when I tell you this.)

O do not count on me for anything,
Although I love you as I do the spring.

—Robert Pack

Definition

This fullness that is emptiness,
This hunger that is food;
This union, solitariness,
This wild air, this warm blood;
This poverty, and rich sensation,
This haste, this slow growing,
True marriage, separation,
All-knowing that is not-knowing;
Late fulfillment, early death,
This huge passion, this small breath.

—May Sarton

Two Kisses

I wear your kiss like a feather
Laid upon my cheek
While I walk the path where the river
Suggests suggests

Dirt off all the streets
Rotting feet of factories.

Swans and boats and corks ride
Elastic waters
The eye is carried by the choppy tide
To a shore opposite of opal-green spaces
The ear is belied
By dreams inside the roar outside.

Between two sailing swans, a light
Stretches on waves, as on your cheek
That other kiss—my life
Waiting for your life to speak.

—Stephen Spender

Unable Are the Loved

Unable are the Loved to die
For Love is Immortality,
Nay, it is Deity—
Unable they that love—to die
For Love reforms Vitality
Into Divinity.

Love—is anterior to Life—
Posterior—to Death—
Initial of Creation, and
The Exponent of Earth—

—Emily Dickinson

Anemone

My eyes are closing, my eyes are opening.
You are looking into me with your waking look.

My mouth is closing, my mouth is opening.
You are waiting with your red promises.

My sex is closing, my sex is opening.
You are singing and offering : the way in.

My life is closing, my life is opening.
You are here.

—Muriel Rukeyser

Letter to P.

Help me to help your life
and so help mine.

Words! Words!

Your needs are children of a past
so strewn with murdered desires
that you must want and want
murderously.

I am willing to be
only a tongue speaking sincerely
the praise your life grows tall on,

the mirror necessary
to render your face its beauty,
your body its splendor,

a sun to light your moon
that otherwise rolls, cold stone,
in darkness, infinitely.

But where I stand
—outside your any recognition of me
who also need
a tongue, a mirror, and a sun—
I cannot help you.

Help me to help you.
I do not utter now
the word ''love.''

—Robert Friend

Happiness of 6 a.m.

Now you come again
Like a very patient ghost,
Offering me Zen records,
A discourse on the stomach
As the seat of the soul,
Your long white neck to kiss.
The tiger's eye that is
Your favorite jewel
Shines in your hand.
Wanting to, I can't conjure
You up, not a touch.
Unbidden, you cross a thousand miles
To say, "This is the gift
I was going to give you forever."

—Harvey Shapiro

Juan's Song

When beauty breaks and falls asunder
I feel no grief for it, but wonder.
When love, like a frail shell, lies broken,
I keep no chip of it for token.
I never had a man for friend
Who did not know that love must end.
I never had a girl for lover
Who could discern when love was over.
What the wise doubts, the fool believes—
Who is it, then, that love deceives?

—Louise Bogan

Seven

We touch.
Shoulder-to-shoulder.
You can't do more when crossing streets
with mannequins in windows looking back.

I try to match your step—
that way I'm sure of staying close.
You smell like love.
That must be so
for what I smell is dear to me and *new*.

And so a little walk through town
becomes a journey
a love vacation from ourselves
but with ourselves.

Everything you say is funny
      or beautiful.

—Rod McKuen

Fifteen

I have loved you
in so many ways
in crowds or alone.
When you were sleeping beside me.
When you were away
and I imagined others watching you in the street
or worse—you in other people's arms.

I have seen the march of beach birds and loved you.
I have lent myself to summer sun and loved you.
And seeing naked trees
            and raising my collar to the wind
and counting minutes till chartered hours were there
I have loved you.

And the questions never asked.
The answers learned at love's expense.
I've promised myself.
I will not ask where you have been tonight
I'll only say hello
            and hope.

—Rod McKuen

Man or Woman   You

man or woman   you   the breath of life
—to find words   that I can   in front of you
over this table   grasping your hands
deliver   looking   straight in your eyes—
words which I will mean   from all within me
and mean so much   that they will writhe   convulse
break bounds   and winging   vigorously clout
the jug of reticence   and crack it
waters to set   warmly   softly   spilling
vibrations   between us   fingertippest
shudders   where we touch each other's quick—
Then   and only then   molding moments
man and woman   you   the breath of life
will know that we   not words   are poetry

—Keith Barnes

Words I

Lightly   it started to rain
A duck skimmed over the mottled lake
We two sat alone

On my solemn lips the wind
froze the warmth of your cradling neck
Your hand withdrew from mine

Words   only words   I had spoken
only   the truth   —I turned to look
and   on your cheek   a tear traced pain

—Keith Barnes

Love Grows Love

Love grows love in the midst of need,
From the dry ground.
Water is a part of the grass, like hope,
And tomorrow is the rebirth of chance:
To gather corn and challenge the sun on a midday,
To gather any day, even in the rain,
To gather me as you would have the world,
Alive, where grown fields and green grass meadows
Are worm-fed, where caterpillars breathe life
To butterflies.

—Hy Sobiloff

Funky Love

We really ought, she said
to be able to stay together
    without making love
        all the time.

Yes, he said smugly
I'm sure it's my fault.

Yes, she said smugly
you smell so greedy
                and good

Swarms and swarms
    of love
        smug, smug, smug.

                —Norman Mailer

The Moment

We passed the ice of pain,
And came to a dark ravine,
And there we sang with the sea;
The wide, the bleak abyss
Shifted with our slow kiss.

Space struggled with time;
The gong of midnight struck
The naked absolute.
Sound, silence sang as one.

All flowed: without, within;
Body met body, we
Created what's to be.

What else to say?—
We end in joy.

—*Theodore Roethke*

Elegy

O lovers cold on mountain drives
    O lovers warm in valleys
O bold loves where the sand flea lives
    O furtive loves in alleys,
featherbeds are dear but sex
    is cheap:
pull your dashboard tight about your necks
    and sleep.

Long are the midnights where the spotlight plays;
soft are the motors of the night patrols;
you love, you dream, you re-rehearse your days:
the boastings by the lockers in the halls,
the maps to where the war is on the walls.

You wish yourself in Canaan or in Carthage
pitching grenades around the sun-struck corners;
you hide behind your books the pulps of carnage
and flip a spitball at the front-bench mourner:
he also dreams of machs and afterburners.

And even those who twist them dream of knives,
and heroes seek their heroes in a book:
the wing-commander shuts his Plutarch's Lives,
the gob his Batman, thug his Captain Hook,
each with the Far Antilles in his look.

Only, where dreams converge, at impact, zero,
a countercurrent takes its pulse, and runs
through troubled worlds of sleep, to you as hero;
and we in bombers, planting sudden suns
that teem upon the earth by megatons—
we in the furrows, spitting fire to windward,
eternally astonished that the wind
spits back—we happy multitude—we kindred
haunters of beaches, mountain drives and blind
alleys—remake the loves we left behind.

White is the flesh entangled in the steel,
thrusting against the dead accelerator:
the moon its timeless lacquer sheds on heel
and trampled skirt alike—on nymph and satyr:
sleep then, within our dream: you dream no greater.

But lovers wake, the spotlight swings,
        the crunch is on the gravel:
start it, gun it, give it wings,
        pull in your ears and travel:
the world is wide God knows, but sex
        is deep:
pull your dashboards tight about your necks
        and sleep.

                                —George Starbuck

Take a Lump of Clay

Take a lump of clay,
Wet it, pat it,
Make a statue of you
And a statue of me.
Then shatter them, clatter them,
Add some water,
And break them and mold them
Into a statue of you
And a statue of me.
Then, in mine, there are bits of you
And in you there are bits of me.
Nothing shall ever keep us apart.

—Kuan Tao Sheng (Sung Dynasty)

From *Love and Lust*

Love is, I think, the most successful attempt to escape
our loneliness and isolation. It is an illusion like every search
for human perfection, but it is the most necessary illusion of
our culture. . . . To connect one's life in thoughts and deeds
with others is the only way to make it worth living

—*Theodor Reik*